SONNETS FROM AESOP

SONNETS FROM AESOP

By Judith Goldhaber

Illustrations by Gerson Goldhaber

RIBBONWEED PRESS
BERKELEY, CALIFORNIA

SONNETS FROM AESOP

Published by
Ribbonweed Press
Berkeley, California
www.sonnetsfromaesop.com

Sonnets from Aesop
Text © 2004 by Judith Goldhaber
Illustrations © 2004 by Gerson Goldhaber
First Edition 2005
Second Printing 2006

ISBN 0-9761554-0-0
Library of Congress Control Number: 2004097118

Cover art: Gerson Goldhaber
Cover design: Dianna LaFerry
Layout & Typesetting: Matt Hoessli, Lazer Image

Printed by Regal Printing Ltd., Hong Kong
Printed in China

For our children

Michaela and Shaya and Nat and Marilyn

and our grandchildren

Ben and Charles and Sam

"Never fear to love" — *Aesop, The Cub and the Kitten*

TABLE OF CONTENTS

2 The Fox, The Cock And The Dog

4 Belling The Cat

6 The Wolf And The Crane

8 The Ass And His Shadow

10 The Shepherd And The Sea

12 The Two Friends And The Bear

14 The Fox And The Grapes

16 Androcles And The Lion

18 The Eagle And The Hawk

20 The Wolf In Sheep's Clothing

22 The Two Pots

24 The Goatherd And The Wild Goats

26 The Shipwrecked Sailors

28 The Dog In The Manger

30 The Bundle Of Sticks

32 The Donkey And The Wolf

34 The Crab And Her Son

36 The Rabbit With Many Friends

38 The Man And His Two Sweethearts

40 The Ass And The Mule

42 The Gluttonous Fox

44 The Peacock And The Crane

46 The Dog And His Reflection

48 The Lion And The Mouse

50 The Boy And The Cookies

52 The Eagle And The Arrow

54 The Wolf And The Sheep

56 The Boasting Traveler

58 The Pig, The Sheep, And The Goat

60 The Rooster And The Jewel

62 The Boy Bathing

64 The Frogs And The Well

66 The Farmer And His Sons

68 The City Mouse And The Country Mouse

70 The Flea And The Ox

72 The Lion, The Fox, And The Ass

74 Hercules And Athena

76 The Seller Of Images

78 The Fox And The Crow

80 The Donkey And The Horse

82 The Dog's House

84 The Fisherman And The Fish

86 The Wolf, The Fox, And The Ape

88 The Crow And The Pitcher

90 The Kingdom Of The Lion

92 The Hare And The Hound

94 The Ant And The Dove

96 The Two Daughters

98 The Fox And The Lion

100 The Stag And The Hunter

102 The Old Woman And The Physician

104 The Serpent And The File

106 The Lark Burying Her Father

108 The Rabbit And The Frogs

110 The Miser

112 The Lion And The Boar

114 The Fox And The Crane

116 The Donkey And The Lapdog

118 The Dog And The Wolf

120 The Old Man And Death

122 The Wolf And The Goat

124 The Lark And Her Young Ones

126 The Ant And The Grasshopper

128 Hercules And The Wagon Driver

130 The Horse, The Deer, And Man

132 The Trees Under The Protection Of The Gods

134 The Lion In Love

136 The Oxen And The Axletrees

138 The Cat And Venus

140 The Wolf And The Kid

142 The Woodsman And The Nightingale

144 The Ant And The Chrysalis

146 The Boy Who Cried Wolf

148 The Horse And His Rider

150 The Fox Who Had Lost His Tail

152 The Hare And The Tortoise

154 The Sick Stag

156 The Milkmaid And Her Pail

158 The Lion, The Fox, And The Beasts

160 The Traveler And Fortune

162 The Stag And The Vine

164 The Peasant And The Eagle

166 The Tree And The Reed

168 The North Wind And The Sun

170 The Hares And The Lions

172 The Salt Merchant And His Donkey

174 The Vixen And The Lioness

176 The Three Tradesmen

178 The Woodsman And The Serpent

180 The Swan And The Goose

182 The Hunter And The Woodsman

184 The Two Friends And The Axe

186 The Fox And The Cat

188 The Silkworm And The Spider

190 The Mule

192 The Lion And The Statue

194 The Cub And The Kitten

196 The Nurse And The Wolf

198 The Frogs Asking For A King

200 The Man, The Boy, And The Donkey

SONNETS

FROM

AESOP

THE FOX, THE COCK
AND THE DOG

"Good news! Good news!" cried a prowling Fox,
"King Lion has declared a worldwide truce!
No beast may hurt another! All abuse
of ducks and geese must stop, and as for flocks
of chickens – well, there's no more need for locks
on henhouse doors! Dear friends, there's no excuse
for roosting up so high! Please don't refuse
to come on down and play!" One of the Cocks
craned his neck sharply toward the barnyard gate,
"Oh good, let's share these tidings with the Dog!
Here he comes now! *What? Leaving?* It's not late!
Do stay and let us hear that dialogue!"
"I would," the Fox cried, as he started running,
"but sometimes I'm outfoxed by my own cunning."

BELLING THE CAT

Once, long ago, a parliament of mice
was summoned to discuss their foe the Cat.
Some of the mice said this and some said that,
and then a young mouse offered this advice:
"The problem with the Cat, to be concise,
is that her footsteps make no pitapat —
she strikes before we realize where she's at!
Let's place around her neck some small device
— a bell, perhaps — that sounds a warning note
when she is near, so we can get away."
The mice applauded this: *"Hip, hip, hooray!*
All those in favor?" "Wait! Before we vote,"
said one old mouse, "who'll place that lavaliere
around her neck? Is there a volunteer?"

THE WOLF AND THE CRANE

Gorging on some poor creature he had slain
a Wolf discovered a bone stuck in his throat.
"I'd pay a fortune for an antidote
or remedy for this horrendous pain!"
he pleaded. "I can help you," bragged a Crane,
"I'm famous for my 'talents' (quote unquote)
in fact, although I do not like to gloat,
I am the model for the term 'birdbrain'!"
"Please," begged the Wolf, "I'll give you all I own!"
And so she thrust her long and supple neck
down the Wolf's throat and grasped the piece of bone.
 "Thanks," said the Wolf, "but don't expect a check,
be glad that you could stick your neck and pull it
back out again from a Wolf's jaws and gullet."

THE ASS AND
HIS SHADOW

Out in the desert there's so little shade
that — though this isn't easy to believe —
travelers often find a brief reprieve
from the harsh sun not in a leafy glade
or in a cooling glass of lemonade
but in the shadow of whatever mammal
is close at hand, be it ass or camel.
One day a traveler in a cavalcade
sought shelter in the shadow of an Ass
that he had hired, but the Ass's master
raced him for the spot, and got there faster.
While they argued over this impasse
the Ass ran off. This story has a moral:
What's real is lost when shadows make us quarrel.

THE SHEPHERD
AND THE SEA

A Shepherd, herding sheep beside the ocean,
beheld a scene so tranquil, blue, and calm
he longed to go to sea. Without a qualm
he sold his sheep, and through a sales promotion
invested in a cargo ship. The motion
of waves grew violent, and a fierce maelstrom
arose, and hit the vessel like a bomb.
The crew survived, but in the wild commotion
the cargo all was lost; yes, every bean
went to the bottom. Later, from a cliff
he watched the Sea again, and mused "What if . . . ?"
but then he thought "Look out! The Sea's serene
today, as smooth as glass, but I don't buy it!
It wants some beans again, and so acts quiet."

THE TWO FRIENDS
AND THE BEAR

Two bosom friends were traveling through a wood
when a Bear rushed out at them. The man in front
seized a nearby branch, and with a grunt
pulled himself to safety. Since he could
not reach the branch, the other fellow stood
his ground, and bravely did confront
the angry Bear, resigned to bear the brunt
of the attack, though in all likelihood
his death was certain. But the Bear embraced
the trembling fellow, pressed his dripping muzzle
against his ear, then turned away. "Now there's a puzzle,"
his friend said, scrambling down the tree post-haste,
"what did he whisper to you in that clinch?"
"Don't trust a friend who dumps you in a pinch."

THE FOX AND
THE GRAPES

The scent of Grapes just ripening on the vine
that clambered up a steep and lofty trellis
attracted a passing Fox. "Feel free to smell us,"
mocked the Grapes, "but if you hope to dine
on us today, I fear you're out of line!
We're way too high to reach, me and my fellas,
so eat your heart out!" Frustrated and jealous,
eventually the Fox had to resign
himself to failure. As he slunk away,
out of breath, his nose up in the air,
"Good riddance to them!" he was heard to say,
"I really can't be bothered, nor do I care!"
Despising that which lay beyond his power
to grasp, he sneered "I'm sure those grapes were sour!"

ANDROCLES AND THE LION

Fleeing from his master's bondage cruel,
the slave Androcles came upon a sight
that gave him the most appalling fright:
a proud and splendid Lion, born to rule
but now brought low, the butt of ridicule,
sprawled on the forest floor in the moonlight.
Feeling a rush of pity for his plight
the slave drew near, and, feeling like a fool,
plucked from the Lion's paw a giant thorn.
Much later, man and Lion met again,
the slave was tossed into the Lion's den,
expecting that to pieces he'd be torn.
The Lion, though, revealed the gratitude
of noble souls, leaving the slave eschewed.

THE EAGLE AND
THE HAWK

A lonely Eagle gave a mournful squawk:
"It's more than I can bear to live alone
without a royal mate to call my own!"
"Take *me*, my queen!" declared an eager Hawk,
"with my sharp eyes and talons I can stalk
the choicest prey to lay before your throne!
Perhaps an ostrich, plump and fully grown?"
"Oh my," the Eagle simpered, *"how you talk!*
A bird so bold should join the royal house!"
And so the Eagle and the Hawk were wed,
but the next morning, in the nuptial bed
he set before his bride a stinking mouse.
"You lied to me," she cried, *"you rotten louse!"*
"It's only proves how highly I esteem you,"
the Hawk said, "that to win you as my spouse
I'd try to pass a mouse off as an emu."

geison

Eagle & Hawk

THE WOLF IN
SHEEP'S CLOTHING

Looking for a suitable disguise
to help him find a cheap and easy meal,
a cunning Wolf decided to conceal
his shaggy coat and gleaming yellow eyes
under a sheepskin, and thus fraternize
with other sheep — (the ones he planned to steal).
The woolly sheepskin costume looked so real
that even the shepherd didn't recognize
the trickster when he shut them in the pen.
The gate was closed, the entrance made secure,
so that no Wolf could penetrate the door.
But when the shepherd boy came back again
to catch and kill a sheep for his *ragout*,
the first one in the pot was you-know-who.

THE TWO POTS

Two Pots were lying on the river bank,
one made of clay, the other made of brass.
The tide rose, and they floated off the grass
into the flood. Neither vessel sank
but rode downstream together, flank by flank.
The Clay Pot cried out "Please don't try to pass
or get too close to me! I'll break like glass
if we collide!" *"Would I play such a prank
on you?"* the Brass Pot scolded, *"I'm your friend!
I'd never strike you! You can count on that!"*
"Alas, it's not a case of tit for tat,"
the Clay Pot said, "My fate does not depend
on who hits whom, or who is in the wrong—
the weak must keep their distance from the strong."

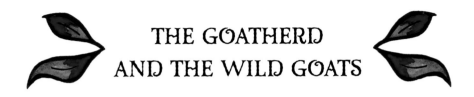

THE GOATHERD
AND THE WILD GOATS

That night the snow came down so thick and hard
a Goatherd was obliged to keep his flock
penned up overnight. At six o'clock
he checked the herd and noticed in the yard
a few Wild Goats, who (when he'd closed and barred
the gate) were trapped. "I've added to my stock!"
the Goatherd gloated, "I wish that I could lock
them up and keep them! Since I can't stand guard
over each Goat, this is what I plan to do!
I'll feed these strangers well, but starve the others,
that way they'll see they are the favored brothers
and stay with me!" But the Wild Goats, who knew
that he who favors new friends over old
cannot be trusted, skedaddled from the fold.

THE SHIPWRECKED
SAILORS

Two shipwrecked sailors on a desert isle
beheld a looming shape on the horizon.
"Come look!" one shouted. "Let us keep our eyes on
that ship! I reckon it's about a mile
away, and we need only wait awhile
before it anchors here to take supplies on."
But as the shape drew near, it shrank in size. On
closer scrutiny, the strange profile
turned out to be no ocean-going schooner
or even a small dinghy or a barge;
in fact, the thing was nothing but a large
bundle of sticks. They should have realized sooner
it doesn't pay to start the celebrations
too soon, since life delights in complications
and often disappoints one's expectations.

THE DOG IN
THE MANGER

The yellow straw that filled the Oxen's manger
looked like a comfy pillow to a Dog.
She stretched out for a snooze, happy to hog
the bed. The Oxen, sensing there'd be danger
when she awoke, and hoping they might change her
attitude (since they were all agog
with fear and hunger) tried a dialogue,
offering to share their dinner with the stranger.
The Dog, though, being wakened from her sleep,
became enraged, and chased the helpless cattle
out of the barn — a most unseemly battle
since dogs would rather dine on pigs or sheep
than straw! But dogs, like men, will oft destroy
the pleasures they themselves cannot enjoy.

THE BUNDLE OF STICKS

An old man nearing his allotted days
was worried that his seven sons were feuding
about their inheritance, including
who should get what, who moves out and who stays,
who must visit whom on holidays
and such important matters. After brooding
about the problem, he formed a plan, concluding
he'd show his sons the folly of their ways.
"Come here, my sons, you'll see a clever trick.
See this bundle of firewood?   Please try
to break it in half!" They struggled to comply,
but soon gave up. *"Now each one take one stick.*
It's easily broken! Sons, you can't go wrong
if you remember union makes us strong."

THE DONKEY AND
THE WOLF

"Uh-oh! I'd better think of something fast!
That Wolf looks like he's on the prowl for game
and that means *me*, and that would be a shame!"
Thus did a Donkey, helpless and aghast,
regard a Wolf pursuing a repast.
The Donkey then pretended to be lame.
"Sir Wolf," he said, "I hope I'm not to blame
for your demise! This day may be your last!
I had a run-in with a porcupine
and if you swallow me you'll get quite ill
trying to digest his buried quill!
Why don't you pluck it out before you dine?"
"Okay, where is it?" asked the Wolf. "Beneath
this hoof!" With that the Donkey kicked him in the teeth
and made his getaway across the heath.

THE CRAB AND
HER SON

"The way you walk, my son, is so erratic
I am ashamed to take you anywhere!"
a mother Crab declared, "I greatly fear
your crooked gait could well be symptomatic
of deeper problems — perhaps something traumatic
in childhood! I don't like to interfere,
but sideways locomotion is so queer!
I recommend a therapy pragmatic:
Do what *I* do, and in no time at all
your footsteps will be just as straight as mine!"
With that, the mother Crab began to crawl
over the sand, tracing a cockeyed line.
"Gee," her son exclaimed, "if *that's* a sample
I promise I will follow your example!"

THE RABBIT WITH
MANY FRIENDS

All of the beasts were friendly with the Rabbit—
the horse, the bull, the goat all called her pal,
she was an easy-going sort of gal,
sincere and loyal, though a trifle drab. It
happened that one day, as was her habit
she was reclining in the chaparral
when startled by a thunderous chorale:
hounds on the scent of prey and set to grab it.
"Dear Friends, please help me! Carry me away
on your broad backs!" *"Oh dear, I'm really busy!"*
"Go ask the horse, he isn't busy, is he?"
"I'd love to help you on another day!"
came the replies from all her so-called cronies.
If you have *lots* of friends, watch out for phonies!

Rabbit with many Friends

THE MAN AND HIS
TWO SWEETHEARTS

A playboy on the downhill side of fifty
whose thick black hair was streaked with strands of gray
courted two women as his fiancée.
The older one was tidy, kind, and thrifty,
the younger one, let's face it, far more nifty
in face and figure. Yet the old roué
adored both women, and saw each every day
(behavior most of us would label shifty).
But his two-timing brought its just desserts!
The older lady, scared that folks would tease her
and brand her as a cradle-robbing flirt,
pulled out his telltale black hairs with her tweezer.
The younger one, ashamed to wed a geezer,
yanked out the gray ones (even though it hurt!).
Looking in the glass, he was appalled
to find that he was now completely bald

The Man and Two Sweethearts

THE ASS AND THE MULE

A certain Mule, half-brother to an Ass,
resented that his mom, a high-born horse,
had practiced unprotected intercourse
with a male donkey. One day it came to pass
both beasts were carrying a load of brass
and silver *chatchkas* from their master's store
up a steep mountain "This burden is much more
than I can bear," the donkey cried, "Alas!
Brother! Please help me with this heavy weight."
"Forget it," said the Mule, "your bro I ain't!"
But when the poor beast fell down in a faint
his master slung the donkey AND his freight
on the Mule's back — a heavy load indeed.
He should have helped his brother in his need!

THE GLUTTONOUS
FOX

Well hidden in the hollow of an oak,
a hungry Fox, peering through a hole in
the massive trunk, saw — begging to be stolen —
a lunch intended for some shepherd folk.
The Fox exulted: "What a lucky stroke!"
Squeezing inside, he stuffed his gut and colon
so greedily his belly soon was swollen
to twice its size. He slept awhile, then woke
and thought, "The time has come for me to crawl out
the hole I entered!" But much to his dismay
his swollen stomach blocked his getaway!
Cursing his fate, the Fox commenced to call out
for help, but all his friends said mockingly
"It looks like you'll be living in that tree
until you are the Fox you used to be!"

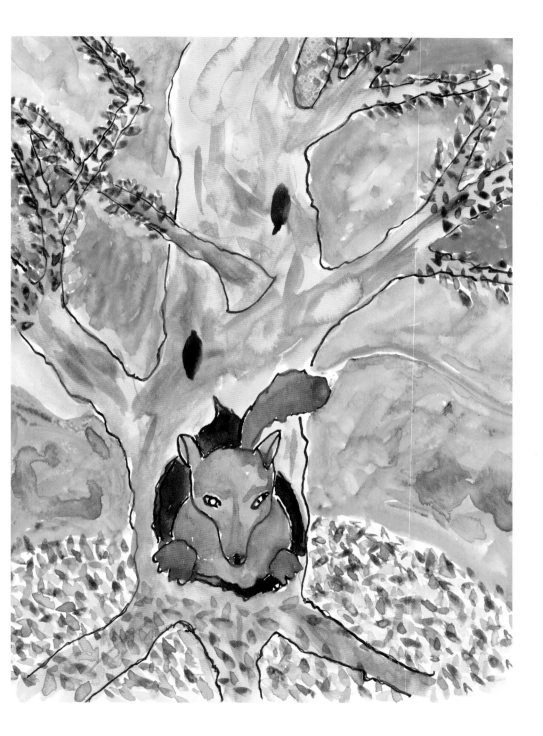

THE PEACOCK
AND THE CRANE

A Peacock, spreading out his gorgeous tail
of gold and purple, tipped with azure plumes,
mocked a passing Crane. "I am abloom
with color, as a potent Alpha Male
should be, but you, my friend, are sickly pale.
You look like you've been sleeping in a tomb!"
"That's true," replied the Crane, "but I presume
you've noticed *I* can *fly*! I don't bewail
my pallor when I climb the lofty heights
of heaven, and sing my carols to the moon,
while you strut here below, deprived of flight —
a cock upon a dunghill, a buffoon
among the pigs and chickens. Mark my words:
It's not fine feathers that define fine birds!"

THE DOG AND
HIS REFLECTION

Crossing a bridge over a woodland creek
while grasping in his jaws a struggling pigeon,
a Dog beheld a most disturbing vision!
Another Dog, of powerful physique,
clutching a bird so big it seemed a freak,
lurked beneath the pillars of the bridge in
anticipation of a fierce collision.
"Stranger, if a fight is what you seek
you'll soon regret you came in my direction!"
he growled, and dropped the pigeon to attack
the other Dog. He never got it back,
because the challenger was his own reflection!
The Dog missed out on two plump birds that day,
one wasn't real, the other flew away.

THE LION AND
THE MOUSE

Imagine the annoyance of the Lion
who woke to find a Mouse upon his face!
The frightened Mouse was quick to make a case
to save his life. "Sir, may I testify in
my own defense? Although you are the scion
of royalty, and I a Mouse (most base
of creatures) there may be a time and place
where *I* can help *you* out, but not by dyin'!"
The king of beasts just laughed, and let him be.
Soon afterwards the Lion got a scare
when wily hunters caught him in a snare;
the Mouse gnawed through the ropes and set him free,
saying, "You doubted I'd repay the favor,
but, now, behold, a Mouse is your lifesaver!"

THE BOY AND
THE COOKIES

Thrusting his hand into the cookie jar,
a greedy urchin stuffed into his fist
all he could hold, but then he found his wrist
was stuck. Exhausting his large repertoire
of expletives, lamenting his bizarre
and gruesome fate, he tried his best to twist
to freedom like a mad contortionist,
but nothing he attempted got him far.
"Alas!" he sobbed, "No matter how I tug
my hand is stuck!" Hearing his lament
his mother said, "You'll wear that cookie jug
until your grave, unless you are content
with fewer cookies! Grasp too much at once,
and you'll go through your life a total dunce!"

THE EAGLE AND
THE ARROW

An Eagle, soaring freely through the air
heard the *whizz* of an arrow's plumèd dart.
It found its mark, and lodged there in his heart;
slowly he fluttered down to earth, aware
that he was dying, "This is so unfair!"
he cried, "No clumsy huntsman could outsmart
an Eagle unless, in his deceitful art,
an Eagle's plumage feathered the fatal spear!"
And so it was: when he looked down upon
his wound, the Eagle saw the arrow's shaft
bore his own gorgeous plume; his epitaph
is one all living things might focus on,
"Alas, dear friends, this is my last instruction:
we give our foes the means for our destruction."

THE WOLF AND
THE SHEEP

"Ah me, I've seen the error of my ways —
a wasted life misspent in selfish slaughter!
If only some kind soul would fetch me water
I'll live on nuts and berries all my days!"
So did a wounded Wolf with honeyed praise
beseech a passing Sheep, but wisdom taught her
to be beware of strangers who besought her
help with empty pledges and clichés.
"What ails you, brother Wolf?" "The hunter's hound
has wounded me! I cannot eat or drink!
But, if you fetch me water, then I think
a way to get my supper might be found."
"I'd like to help," the Sheep replied, "but when you
have slaked your thirst and are yourself again you
are sure to put roast lamb back on the menu!"

The Wolf and the Sheep

THE BOASTING
TRAVELER

A man who'd traveled round the world and back,
on coming home again could not refrain
from pouring out his scorn on the mundane
lives of his friends, and pitying their lack
of daring exploits. "I just have the knack
of doing things that most men can't attain!
I jumped a hundred feet or more in Spain!"
So on and on this egomaniac
described his awesome feats of derring-do,
his splendid physical and mental fitness,
saying "Don't take my word! I have a witness
in Spain who'll swear that what I say is true!"
"No need for witnesses," spoke up one kid,
"go take a flying leap, pretend it's Madrid!"

THE PIG, THE SHEEP, AND THE GOAT

Once on a farm a friendly Goat and Sheep
shared their enclosure with a surly Pig
who bragged "They'll never keep me in this brig!"
Whenever the farmer petted him, he'd leap
out of his arms, and once he tried to creep
under the fence (alas! he was too big).
One night he found a spot where he could dig
a hole, and when the barnyard was asleep
he wriggled through, pausing to say goodbye
to his old friends, who said, "Why make a fuss?
The farmer often pets and handles *us*!"
"He wants something from you," came the reply,
"milk for his children, warm wool for his wife,
but all that *I* can give him is my life!"

THE ROOSTER AND
THE JEWEL

Scratching for his breakfast in the yard
among the pebbles, chaff, and other litter,
a Rooster found a stone that seemed to glitter.
His inclination was to disregard
the little thing as just another shard
of broken glass. "I can't afford to fritter
my time away," he grumbled, feeling bitter.
But just as he was ready to discard
the shiny stone, he saw it was a jewel —
a diamond worthy of an emperor's crown.
"Alas," he pondered as he tossed it down,
"fate is capricious, and it can be cruel!
Although a monarch's brow you might adorn
I'd gladly trade you for one barleycorn."

THE BOY BATHING

Over his head in water deep and cold
a hapless Boy was close to being drowned.
A passerby, attracted by the sound
of desperate cries, with hands in pockets strolled
down to the lake, where he commenced to scold
the wretched youth. *"You reckless scamp!"* he frowned,
*"with boys like you this sort of thing is bound
to happen!"* "Please sir, don't withhold
your help!" the Boy exclaimed. "Give me your hand
and let me hear the lecture later on!
Your words won't matter much when I am gone!"
From this fable we should understand
a helping hand is better than abuse,
and counsel without help is not much use.

THE FROG AND
THE WELL

No rain for months, and unrelenting drought
where once it used to rain like cats and dogs
dried up the once luxuriant woodland bogs.
"You know, it's clear that we had best get out
of here directly, or without a doubt,
we'll die along with all our pollywogs,"
decreed the august council of the Frogs.
And so they sent a frog ahead to scout
the forest for a place where they might move.
Soon he returned: "I found a nice deep well!
Let's jump right in! A perfect place to dwell!"
But one Frog piped up: "Whoa! I don't approve!
Suppose the *well* dries up? If it's so deep,
can we jump *out*? Let's look before we leap!"

THE FARMER
AND HIS SONS

"Come close, my Sons, and hear my final words —
I wish to leave my wealth in equal measure
to my three Sons, and it would give me pleasure
to know my fields, my vineyards, and my herds
are not neglected . . . now and afterwards.
Therefore, my Sons, I've buried a rich treasure
under the vineyard. Dig, and, at your leisure
when I am gone, divide the prize in thirds."
Thus did a Farmer, at the point of death,
address his Sons, who willingly obeyed
and tilled the soil with hoe and plow and spade
as soon as he had drawn his final breath.
And though they never did find any loot,
the vines repaid them with abundant fruit.

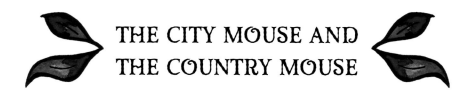

THE CITY MOUSE AND
THE COUNTRY MOUSE

A country weekend — sunshine and fresh air! —
sounded attractive to an urban Mouse
who lived in a deluxe apartment house
near Piccadilly, when his old confrere
the Country Mouse invited him to share
his burrow. But he soon commenced to grouse
about the lousy food and flatulent cows.
He grumbled "Country living can't compare
with my lush life at home! Come to the city
with me, and we will dine on caviar
(a specialty of the trash can in the bar)!"
His friend replied: "But what about the kitty,
the poison, and the traps? No, I'll stay here,
where I can live in safety, without fear!"

City Mouse & Country Mouse

THE FLEA AND
THE OX

"What ails you, brother Ox?" a spunky Flea
rebuked his friend. "You bear without objection
or any thought of violent insurrection
the burdens that men place on you! But me,
I say bite 'em! Bite 'em ruthlessly!
I may be tiny, but my predilection
is human blood! It suits me to perfection!"
"I would not want to change my destiny;
my master treats me well," replied the Ox,
"I like it when he smiles and pats my shoulder."
"Kindness is in the eye of the beholder!"
the Flea snapped back, "how's this for paradox?
That well-intentioned pat for which *you* wished
just means that *I* am going to get squished."

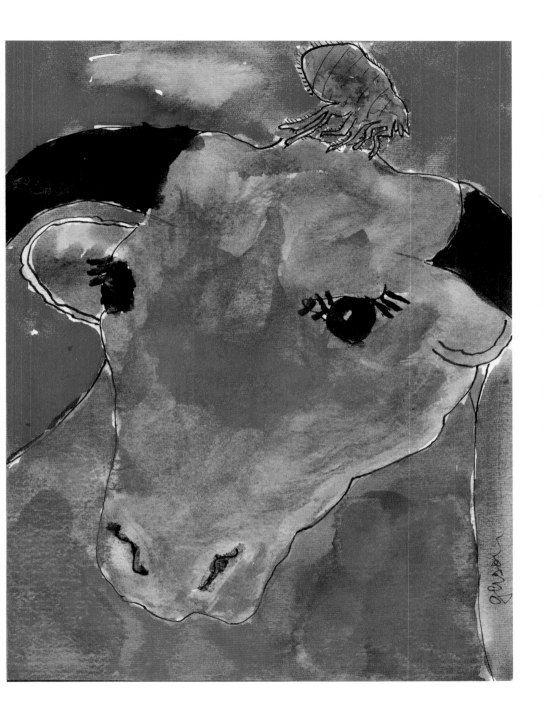

THE LION, THE FOX, AND THE ASS

As equal partners in a solemn pact
an Ass, a Fox, and a Lion all agreed
to help each other out in time of need
and hunt their prey together. The contract
made clear that the division be exact,
with equal share of spoils to each; indeed
Lion and Fox did graciously concede
that duty to the Ass, who did the act
then urged the Lion to make the first selection.
Enraged, the Lion devoured the hapless Ass.
The Fox's turn to choose came next, "I pass,"
he said. "Please, sire, take the whole collection!"
(He'd learned the rules of how to allocate
from Professor Ass, by witnessing his fate.)

The Lion the Fox & the Ass

HERCULES AND ATHENA

Driving his chariot on a narrow road
Hercules was threatened by a beast
that reared its head as if to make a feast
of him. Undaunted, the intrepid hero strode
ahead, and struck the creature with his goad.
Instead of slinking off, the thing increased
ten times in size, until it filled at least
half of the highway. Then Athena showed
herself upon the scene. "O, stop your blows
dear Hercules, put down your sword and knife!
They do no good! This monster's name is Strife!
It feeds on conflict, so do not oppose
its strength by force of arms. Leave it alone
and it will fade away all on its own."

THE SELLER OF IMAGES

A craftsman who carved wooden statuettes
of Mercury, the god of trade and cunning,
was vexed because the customers were shunning
his wares, while his expenses and his debts
kept mounting. *"Are you sick of tradesmen's threats?"*
he advertised, *"Do creditors keep dunning*
you for money? Have you considered running?
Here's help, my friends! Now triple your assets!
Get wealthy just by praying to this carving!"
But someone griped "I don't believe your pitch!
Why sell it, if that thing can make you rich?"
"Right now," the man replied, "my kids are starving!
The gods, though potent, tend to be capricious —
they take their time in granting mortals' wishes."

THE FOX AND
THE CROW

A Crow, having filched a piece of meat,
perched in a treetop to enjoy the meal.
A passing Fox, thinking that he might steal
the treasure, devised a plan to cheat
the Crow by playing on her conceit.
"How lovely is the Crow, and how ideal
the beauty of her figure! Her appeal
would be sublime if only her voice were sweet!"
*"My voice? What's wrong with it? There is no flaw
in my perfection!"* thought the foolish Crow.
Seeing the Fox waiting patiently below
she spread her beak in a resounding *"CAW!"*
"You're right," the Fox replied, "your voice is fine,
your wit's what's wanting, and the meat is mine!"

gerson

THE DONKEY AND
THE HORSE

A Donkey, sharing quarters with a Horse,
begged him to share a portion of his feed —
barley and oats and corn. The highborn steed
looked down his nose at him and said, "Of course!
My status and my breeding reinforce
my natural sympathy for those in need —
'Help the downtrodden' is my sacred creed!"
So on and on went this high-flown discourse;
meanwhile the donkey, flirting with starvation
had not a bite to eat. "Please, sir," he said,
"your views are noble, but I may be dead
before you have completed your oration!
Just offer me a few oats here and now,
and you can keep your sanctimonious vow!"

Donkey + Horse

THE DOG'S HOUSE

Shivering through a frigid winter night,
a Dog curled up his body in a ball
and squeezed into a space extremely small.
Freezing, he resolved to ease his plight
by fashioning a dog house, snug and tight,
just big enough, measured wall to wall,
to keep him cozy in next winter's squall.
But when sweet summer brought its warmth and light,
the Dog stretched out to bask beneath the sun.
"I say," he marveled, "here's a funny puzzle!
I've grown quite long from tip of tail to muzzle!
It's just as well I haven't yet begun
to build that dog house; I'd just have to quit,
since anyone can see I wouldn't fit!"

THE FISHERMAN
AND THE FISH

Hearing that music casts a magic spell
that makes fish dance, a crafty Fisherman
stood beside the seashore and began
to play his bagpipes at a decibel
loud enough to rouse the souls in hell.
But no fish rose. *"I'll try another plan*
to get these fish into my frying pan.
I'll cast my net in waters where they dwell!"
And so he cast his net into the sea
and drew it up abrim with thrashing fish.
"O perverse creatures, NOW you grant my wish
and dance within my net so merrily!"
"One must," a Fish replied, "when on the griddle,
dance to the tune of he who plays the fiddle."

THE WOLF, THE FOX,
AND THE APE

A Wolf accused his neighbor Fox of stealing,
although the Fox denied the accusation.
At last the parties sought adjudication
before an Ape, with each of them appealing
for justice while all the time concealing
his own deceptions and prevarication.
When each of them had finished his oration
the verdict of the Ape sent both beasts reeling.
"I do not think *you*, Wolf, lost what you claim,
but *you*, sir Fox, have most assuredly stolen
what you deny. Your stories both are lame,
and far be it from me to play a role in
this travesty! I say you're both to blame!"
Their howls of protest were of no avail —
Wolf and Fox both spent the night in jail.

THE CROW AND
THE PITCHER

Bedraggled, sore, and perishing with thirst,
a Crow was looking for a place to die
when suddenly a miracle caught his eye:
an earthen Pitcher, holding the very first
water he'd seen since April's last cloudburst —
a few drops only, reflecting the azure sky
but out of reach despite his every try.
"Shall I give up and count myself accursed,
since all my efforts seem to be in vain
or should I hunker down and use my brain?"
Some scattered pebbles caught the Crow's attention:
one by one he dropped them in the vase:
the water rose — proof that persistence pays
and desperate need is mother of invention.

THE KINGDOM
OF THE LION

The beasts of field and forest had as king
a kindly Lion, neither cold nor cruel
nor harsh, but one who based his gentle rule
on justice, and who hated anything
that marred the peace, like petty arguing
among his subjects. He outlawed ridicule,
and sent repeat offenders back to school
to learn to live without belittling
each other. Then the king proclaimed a union
wherein the weak and strong (the Wolf and Lamb,
the Hound and Hare, the Seagull and the Clam)
would live as one in comradely communion.
"My dream come true! A world that's free of strife!"
the Hare exclaimed, while running for his life.

THE HARE AND
THE HOUND

Emerging for a moment from her lair
to beat the bushes for her daily ration
of heather, grass, and other vegetation
around her forest home, a timid Hare
was spotted by a Hound. At once the pair
took up the chase. Propelled by desperation,
her legs the only ticket to salvation,
she soon showed her pursuer her derriere.
 At last the tired Hound gave up the chase.
"That little Hare has beat you by a mile!"
jeered a passing shepherd with a smile.
The Hound retorted, "Sir, in any race
even a fool like you can pick the winner
when one runs for his life, one for his dinner."

THE ANT AND
THE DOVE

On a branch overhanging rushing water,
preening her feathers, sat a turtledove.
Looking down from her safe perch above
the torrent, she beheld a pending slaughter:
an Ant was drowning where the current caught her.
Plucking a large leaf from a tall foxglove
the kind bird tossed it; with a little shove
the Ant climbed on, and soon the green boat brought her
safely to shore. Pausing to catch her breath
the Ant espied a huntsman with his bow
aimed at the Dove; she bit him in the toe,
the shot went wide, the Dove escaped her death
and quickly flew away. From this we learn
the good we do will bring us good in turn.

THE TWO
DAUGHTERS

A merchant had two Daughters, both adored
and pampered by their father and his wife.
One wed a gardener, the other joined her life
to a bricklayer. Fearful of discord,
the loving parents showed their favor toward
each girl in equal measure, and yet strife
broke out and split the family like a knife.
It happened when the gardener's wife implored
her father, "If you love me, pray for rain!"
The other begged her mother, "Pray for sky
of blue, and sunshine, so the bricks can dry!"
"My dears," they told their Daughters, "please refrain!
The gods will regulate their own affairs
no matter whom we favor in our prayers!"

THE FOX AND
THE LION

Terribly frightened by the lordly beast
who stood before him, a Fox beheld the King
of all the animals, the Lion, in the spring.
The yellow eyes, the jaws, the claws, unleashed
such fear in him he scurried off like greased
lightning, not stopping till he reached the sheltering
haven of the woods, worn out and shivering.
By Easter time his courage had increased,
and now he watched the Lion, a voyeur
at a safe distance. At last, when summer came
he boldly called the Lion by his name
and sniggered "Ain't you hot in all that fur?"
which proves that close acquaintance breeds contempt,
and even the king of beasts is not exempt.

THE STAG AND
THE HUNTER

Admiring his image in a forest stream
where he had stopped to drink, a noble Stag
couldn't resist the tendency to brag
about his spreading antlers. "How they gleam!
They are my golden crown! My legs, though, seem
(though good enough for leaping crag to crag)
a tad too thin! To tell the truth, they drag
down my appearance and my self-esteem!"
But fortune had in store a lesson grim:
An arrow whistled by; the Stag took flight
on nimble legs and soon was out of sight;
then in a fir tree's overhanging limb
his antlers tangled, and he learned too late
that what's most useful is often what we hate.

THE OLD WOMAN
AND THE PHYSICIAN

A doctor once was called upon to treat
a rich Old Woman who was going blind.
This is the contract that both parties signed:
If he restored her vision (quite a feat!)
she'd pay, but if the cure was incomplete
he wouldn't get a dime. He didn't mind
those terms, since the good doctor was inclined
to pay himself by practicing deceit,
stealing her goods each time he paid a call.
At last, when there was nothing left to steal
he cured her, saying "Ma'am, we made a deal,
so pay me!" Said the lady: "Not at all!
If I'm no longer blind, as you declare,
why can't I see the stuff I know is there?"

THE SERPENT AND
THE FILE

"Take that! And that! You insignificant slab
of rusting iron! How dare you prick my skin?
Now you see the angry mood I'm in!
Notice my weapons — curving fangs that stab
my foe while shooting poison with each jab,
constricting coils that crush the life within;
so if you want to fight, I'm bound to win
and there'll be no one left alive to blab!"
Thus did a Serpent, frustrated and furious,
unleash his fury on an iron File.
But wise Athena told him, "Save your bile;
nothing you say or do can be injurious
to iron. Though your rage is comprehensible,
it's useless to beat up on the insensible."

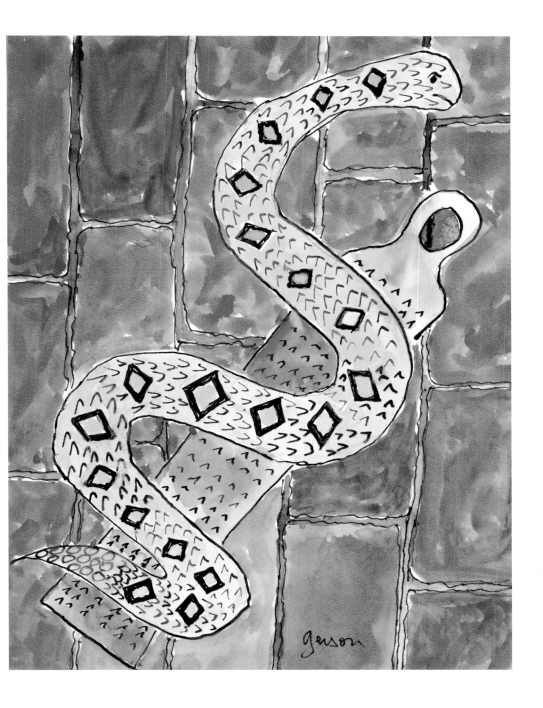

THE LARK BURYING
HER FATHER

Even before the world we know was made,
while formless darkness lingered on the deep
and the Earth's past and future lay asleep,
Zeus made the Larks. They sang their serenade
and tumbled through the vacuum unafraid.
But one day Zeus beheld a young Lark weep.
"Master, there is a promise I must keep
to my dead father, lest he feel betrayed.
All living creatures need to mourn their dead
and hide their bones with reverence in the ground,
but no fit place of burial have I found
though twice as far as Arcturus I have sped!"
To honor her devotion, Zeus made the Earth:
so one Lark's death became our green globe's birth.

THE RABBIT AND
THE FROGS

The Rabbit was an apprehensive fellow,
living in a constant state of manic
depression; his own shadow made him panic,
the scent of foxes turned his legs to jello,
and if he chanced to hear a bull moose bellow
his body trembled with a shock galvanic.
The power of his fear was so volcanic
even his closest buddies called him yellow.
Crouched in the reeds along the riverside
the Rabbit contemplated suicide,
but when he plunged into the swirling tide
a troop of green Frogs scuttled off, bug-eyed
with terror. As his chest puffed up with pride,
the Rabbit thought, "I'll live with dignity
now that I know that someone's scared of *me*!"

THE MISER

A rich man owned a vineyard and a farm
and herds of cattle. All of these he sold
one day to buy a heavy lump of gold.
The threat of robbers filled him with alarm
and so to keep his treasure safe from harm
he hid it six feet underground, and rolled
a stone to mark the place. He never told
a soul where it was stashed, and, to disarm
suspicion, dined on scraps and dressed in tatters,
but every day he paid his hoard a visit.
One day the gold was gone! He cried *"Where is it?"*
"You never used it, so it hardly matters,"
a wise friend told him. "There's no need to grieve,
just bury a stone instead, and make believe
the gold's still lying there, untouched by thieves."

THE LION AND
THE BOAR

Arguing over who should get to drink
first from a well, there rose a fierce dispute
between Lion and Boar. Each grimly resolute
in his defiance, neither beast would shrink
from argument, or draw back from the brink.
And so in bloody combat, brute to brute,
with neither giving ground in his pursuit,
they fought all day, since neither one would blink.
As night came on they paused to catch their breath
and noticed roosting in a nearby tree
a dark shape, waiting oh so patiently
for one of them to tumble down to death.
At once they made their peace, aware that culture
owes its existence to the hovering vulture.

THE FOX AND
THE CRANE

A Fox once asked a Crane to come to dinner
just for the fun of making her a dupe
and laughingstock, because the meal was soup—
a diet sure to make a Crane grow thinner!
Each time the poor Crane tried to put it in her,
it dribbled from her beak like greasy goop!
All this was quite amusing to the group
of dinner guests, who crowned the Fox the winner
and King of Nasty Jokes by acclamation.
But when the Crane returned the invitation
she planned a trick to fix the Fox's wagon.
The food was served inside a thin-necked flagon,
giving the hungry Fox acute frustration.
His meal of fragrant rabbit stew was wasted,
and his own medicine was all he tasted.

THE DONKEY AND
THE LAPDOG

"O for the life of Master's little poodle!"
a discontented Donkey once complained;
"she's fed with loving care, and entertained
with toys, while I must labor under brutal
conditions that are best described as feudal!"
One day the Donkey jumped the fence and gained
its freedom, and with rapture unrestrained
galloped to the house. "Now *I'll* canoodle
and fawn and caper like that stupid dog,
and when I'm tired I'll just take a nap!"
With that, it jumped into its Master's lap
and licked his face. Alas, the epilogue
to this adventure proves it's hard to pass
for something that you're not, if you're an ass.

THE DOG AND
THE WOLF

A gaunt Wolf, almost dying of starvation,
met a house Dog who was passing by.
"Ah, Cousin," said the Dog, "you can't deny
this life you lead is full of aggravation,
and since you are my closest blood relation
I'd like to help! Perhaps you should apply
for steady work, like me! You'll get a dry
place to sleep and ample daily ration
of food to eat." "I would have no objection,"
the Wolf replied. "But what's the reason, pray,
the hair upon your neck's so worn away?"
"My master, as a sign of his affection,
places round my neck a sturdy collar
and chains me up at night for my protection."
"No thanks," the Wolf replied, "I'll live in squalor
before I sell my freedom for a dollar."

THE OLD MAN
AND DEATH

The ten-mile journey from the woods to town
became too wearisome for an old Woodcutter,
"This is no way to earn my bread and butter
in my old age," he sighed, *"I think I'll drown*
myself!" With that he threw his heavy burden down.
"Come get me, Death!" No sooner did he utter
those words than with a rumble and a flutter
Death sat beside him, asking with a frown
"You called for me, old man? What's on your mind?"
"Oh, nothing much," the Woodcutter replied,
"certainly no big thing like suicide!
I only ask, if you would be so kind,
please lift my load, since I am getting older,
and place it once again upon my shoulder."

THE WOLF AND
THE GOAT

At the top of a rocky precipice
a mountain Goat was grazing in the grass.
A gray Wolf, watching her, called out "Alas
my dear, I fear you'll fall into the abyss
if you're not careful! Don't take it amiss
if I suggest you move from that crevasse
down to this idyllic mountain pass.
This tender meadow grass is perfect bliss!
"I must admit the grass down there looks greener"
the Goat replied, "and you are very kind
to point this out, and yet, if you don't mind,
there's something in your courteous demeanor
that indicates (and please don't think me rude!)
that it's *yourself* who is in want of food."

THE LARK AND HER YOUNG ONES

Living all summer in the tall green wheat
of a farmer's field, a Lark and her young brood
never lacked for camouflage or food.
One day September's chill replaced the heat
of August, and the crop was ripe to eat.
The farmer then approached a multitude
of friends and neighbors. "Much obliged if you'd
help with the harvest, we'll get it done *toute suite*!"
"Eeek, Mama!" loudly squalled the baby chicks,
"we've gotta move! Our nest will be destroyed!"
"Calm down," she yawned, "let's not get paranoid.
He's asked his friends to help him! Fiddlesticks!
The time to get concerned about our health
is when he says 'I'll do the job myself'!"

THE ANT AND
THE GRASSHOPPER

Chirping and singing to his heart's delight
all through one summer's term from dewy morn
to burnished sunset in the golden corn,
a Grasshopper, just to be polite
thought it only proper to invite
a passing Ant, burdened and careworn
with sheaves of grain too heavy to be borne
to join him as a happy sybarite.
"Why work so hard, when life is meant for play?"
The Ant could not approve this attitude:
"When winter comes, what will you do for food?"
 he glumly muttered, as he crawled away.
The Ant was right, of course, and so must we
 in sunlight plan for dark necessity.

HERCULES AND
THE WAGON DRIVER

A Wagon Driver on a muddy road
found that his wheels were sinking in the mire.
The situation quickly became dire —
the horses strained beneath the heavy load,
the Wagon Driver lashed them with his goad,
to no avail. "It's clear that I require
divine assistance now!" he cried out. "Sire!
Hercules! I, who worship you, am owed
a favor! Help me now in my distress!
O Hercules! I have no friend but thee!"
he importuned the god on bended knee.
"Twas you who got yourself into this mess,"
the god replied, "I'm deaf to your appeal —
Get up and put your shoulder to the wheel!"

THE HORSE, THE DEER, AND MAN

Long ago, horses claimed as their domain
all meadows lush with green and tender grass,
but after many years it came to pass
that deer moved down from mountains to the plain
to share the pasture. Then did a Horse complain
loudly to Man, and begged him to harass
these interlopers daring to trespass
on meadowlands where horses used to reign.
"Sure, but you'll have to carry me, because
deer run so fast!" said Man. "Why don't I straddle
your back? Hold still while I adjust this saddle
and place this iron bit between your jaws."
"I reckon that's okay," replied the horse,
"but *just this once*, and only to pursue
those deer! Then take them off!" Said Man "Of course!"
(cinching the girth) "Now, would I lie to you?"

Horse Deer & Man 06   gerson

THE TREES UNDER THE PROTECTION OF THE GODS

The ancient gods conferred unique protection
on certain trees. Cybele chose the pine,
Venus the myrtle, Jupiter — divine
lord of all the gods — pledged his affection
to the oak tree; Apollo claimed connection
with the laurel, and Hercules built his shrine
of sturdy poplar. Then did the benign
and wise Minerva utter an objection:
"Why scorn the humble trees that bring forth fruit?"
"We would not wish for men to think us needy
of nourishment, like mortals weak and greedy."
"Pooh!" said Minerva (typically astute),
"I choose the olive, stunted, gnarled, and plain;
unless a thing has use, its glory's vain."

Trees under Protection of the Gods

THE LION IN LOVE

A lovesick Lion sought the hand in marriage
of a fair maiden, a young and tender thing.
Her parents had no wish to have the king
of beasts as son-in-law, but to disparage
the Lion's suit might bring about a trage-
dy, and so the father turned to faking.
"Sire," he said, "your passionate love-making
might be too rough, and do our daughter damage,
therefore, I humbly venture to suggest
you have your teeth extracted, and your paws
improved by the removal of those claws!"
The eager Lion granted their request,
but when he came to claim his mademoiselle
the parents laughed, and bade him go to hell.

THE OXEN AND
THE AXLETREES

One day a team of overburdened Oxen
was dragging a cart along a country lane;
the Axle groaned as if it were in pain
each time the wagon lurched against the rocks in
the stony path. "Hey," cried the Oxen's coxswain,
"I beg you kindly, Axle, to refrain
from all that screeching, since it's pretty plain
that *we're* the ones receiving the hard knocks in
this situation! If anyone makes a fuss
and cries to heaven for the pain he feels,
it shouldn't be the axle and the wheels
groaning and grumbling, it should be *us*!"
This lesson shows in nature, man or beast,
that those who suffer most cry out the least.

THE CAT AND VENUS

Cupid's arrow strikes where'er it will,
and so a Cat (a tabby, red and white)
fell deeply, hopelessly, in love, despite
the fact that he who gave her heart a thrill
was a handsome young Man — a strange and bitter pill
for her to swallow. The Cat's romantic plight
touched the heart of Venus, who, to unite
the lovers, used her transforming skill
to change the Cat into a maiden fair.
The former kitty was a happy bride
until the day a mouse ran by her chair.
After she ate it, she felt mortified,
but all the laws of gods and legislatures
are powerless against our inner natures.

THE WOLF AND
THE KID

Perched atop a house, a boastful Kid
(not the human species, but a goat)
looked down and saw a Wolf. *"Hey, you! Cutthroat!*
Assassin! Thief! I solemnly forbid
you to pass by here, after what you did!
And tell your pals the weasel and the stoat
to watch their backs! The noose or the garrote
await them when I find out where they've hid!"
"Curse away all you like, my callow friend,"
the Wolf replied, "Pile on the metaphors
and insults against all the carnivores!
We'd hear you better, though, if you'd descend!
Let's see how bold you are with coexistence —
It's easy to be brave from a safe distance!"

THE WOODSMAN AND
THE NIGHTINGALE

Charmed and enchanted through a summer night
by the rapturous singing of a Nightingale,
a Woodsman set a trap beside the trail
and caught the hapless singing bird in flight.
"Now I have caught thee, and to my delight
thou'll sing for *me*," he said. "Let's hear a scale!"
"Nightingales don't ever sing in jail,"
the bird replied, "but if you treat me right
you'll learn three secrets!" So he set it free.
When safely perched upon the highest bough
it warbled: "*One*: Don't trust a captive's vow;
Two: Keep the bird you have in hand; and *Three*:
Don't waste your tears on what is gone for good!"
With that, the bird flew off into the wood.

THE ANT AND
THE CHRYSALIS

Stretching its six legs on a summer day
an Ant crawled onto something stiff and strange:
a Chrysalis close to its time of change.
Imprisoned in its intricate glacé
carapace, the silent creature lay
unmoving. "God forbid that I exchange
my life for yours, since I am free to range
wherever I choose!" the Ant sneered as it staggered on its way.
Soon afterwards the Ant was crawling by
that place again, and found an empty shell
there on the ground. "I wonder what befell
that ugly *thing*," it asked a butterfly
fanning its wings nearby. "Now learn your lesson,
O foolish Ant — don't judge by first impression."

THE BOY WHO
CRIED WOLF

A lonely Shepherd tending to his sheep
high on a mountain in Afghanistan
devised a quite imaginative plan
to get some folks to climb up to the steep
meadow where he spent his days, and keep
him company. Leaving the flock, he ran
down to the village, shouting so every man,
woman, and child was roused from peaceful sleep.
"Wolf! Wolf! he cried (*though really there was none!*)
The people all rushed out to give him aid
in his distress; of course, they felt betrayed
when they found out that it was all in fun!
Seeing that he'd become a laughingstock
the townsfolk yawned and muttered *"Poppycock!"*
the next day, when a real Wolf ate the flock.

THE HORSE AND
HIS RIDER

The Rider of a proud and gallant steed
who'd borne him safely through the fiercest battle
never thought to treat his Horse as chattel,
but tended gladly to its every need,
from cozy stall to oats and corn for feed
and fancy decorations for its saddle.
But when the war was over, he said "That'll
do for you, my spoiled and pedigreed
old friend!" From that day on he fed it chaff
and made it pull a plow like any farmer.
But war broke out again, and, clad in armor,
he mounted the Horse, who with a hollow laugh
collapsed and gasped, "Your noble steed's *kaput*!
I guess you'll have to fight this war on foot!"

THE FOX WHO HAD
LOST HIS TAIL

A Fox who got his tail caught in a trap
escaped the trap, but left the tail behind;
"*Oh-oh*," he thought, "my friends will not be kind
when they behold this puny little flap
on my rear end; it's quite a handicap!
A Fox without a tail will be maligned
and ridiculed, but what I have in mind
should turn the tables on this sad mishap!"
He told his friends "Oh boy, am I in luck!
I finally got rid of that big furry
brush — so awkward when you're in a hurry,
and quite unhealthy, trailing in the muck."
"A fine tale, but no matter how you spin it
I don't believe a single word that's in it,"
a wise fox said, "I'm sure if you could pin it
back on your rump, you'd do so in a minute!"

THE HARE AND
THE TORTOISE

"Hey, Stumpy! Is that you or just some rock?"
a rude Hare ridiculed his friend the Tortoise.
"Are you alive, or is that rigor mortis?"
The Tortoise answered, "Go ahead and mock,
you think it's fun to make a laughingstock
of me! Well, that's what your idea of sport is!
But never mind how difficult or short is
the course, I'll race with you against the clock!"
And so the two agreed to have a race.
Far out in front after the opening lap
the Hare reflected, "Why not take a nap?"
The Tortoise kept a slow but steady pace,
and when he crossed the finish line with ease
the Hare was way behind, still catching ZZZZZZZ's.

THE SICK STAG

"We came as soon as we received your cable!"
"Dear friend, so sorry that you're feeling ill!"
"Take it easy now, don't catch a chill!"
"We'll help in any way that we are able!"
So did the self-styled friends in this old fable,
full of fake compassion and goodwill,
address an ailing Stag with voices shrill
while helping themselves to tidbits from his table.
So many came to pray for his salvation
(with each one taking "just a bite" of food
while they expressed sincere solicitude)
the poor Stag soon expired from starvation.
To those who read these words it should be plain
that bad companions bring more hurt than gain.

THE MILKMAID AND
HER PAIL

A pretty Milkmaid, balancing her Pail
of milk from field to farmhouse, fell to musing
about how she would spend the summer, using
the money she expected from the sale
of all that milk. "No way my plan can fail,"
she thought: "First I'll acquire some chickens, choosing
only the finest brooding hens. Then, losing
no time, I'll sell a thousand eggs retail
at a huge profit! Then I'll buy a gown
to wear to parties! When the boys propose
I'll gaze at them disdainfully down my nose
and toss my head *like this!*" The Pail fell down,
the milk all spilled. So victory is snatched
from she who counts her chicks before they're hatched.

THE LION, THE FOX, AND THE BEASTS

A Lion once announced that he was dying —
beyond the help of remedy or pill.
"Dear friends," he said, "I fear I'm much too ill
to venture forth; instead," he whispered, sighing,
"come see me in the cave where I am lying
to hear the reading of my final will;
you may be mentioned in a codicil."
Soon sheep and goats and cattle were all vying
to gain admittance to the Lion's den.
But not the Fox. He stood outside the door.
"Come in, come in," the Lion urged again.
The Fox replied, "My Liege, I'm keeping score;
I count a lot of footprints going in,
but none come out. I think I'll save my skin!"

THE TRAVELER
AND FORTUNE

Just looking for a place to lay his head,
not realizing he was a sitting duck
for any passing motor car or truck,
a tired Traveler placed his makeshift bed
beside the road. "At this rate you'll be dead
by morning, and the world will say *'Bad luck!'*
since mortals always like to pass the buck
to me, when they should blame themselves instead!"
It was Dame Fortune who addressed him thus,
shaking him roughly till he was awake
"I beg you, for your safety and my sake,
go find a spot to sleep less dangerous,
for men are sure to blame your woes on *me*,
when really *you* control your destiny!"

THE STAG AND
THE VINE

A Stag who'd had his fill of being chased
by huntsmen, hid himself beneath a Vine,
imploring, "Please, I beg of you, entwine
your leaves around me till I am encased
and safe from the catastrophe I faced."
To which the Vine (by temperament benign)
replied "You're safe with me, I can't decline
to help a fellow creature!" and embraced
the trembling Stag. The danger seemed averted!
But then the Stag thought, "It would be a waste
to leave this tender Vine without a taste!"
and nibbled on a leaf. The crunch alerted
the hunters, and they galloped back post haste.
"It serves me right!" the Stag, while fleeing, blurted.
"To dine upon that Vine was *so* perverted!
I should have thanked it, and instead I hurt it!"

THE PEASANT AND
THE EAGLE

This is the story of a kindly Peasant
who stopped to give assistance to an Eagle
caught in a snare. "It ought to be illegal
to trap this noble creature like a pheasant
or crow! Begone! I'm making you a present
of freedom!" And with that he let the regal
king of birds fly free as any seagull
riding the ocean breeze. "Well, that was pleasant!
Now for a snooze!" But then he heard a racket —
the Eagle, swooping down, let fall a pebble
which landed on his skull as if to crack it!
"Is this the thanks I get, ungrateful devil?"
he shouted as he bolted upright, leaping
just as the wall collapsed where he'd been sleeping.

THE TREE AND
THE REED

In accents ripe with scorn and condescension
a stately Tree addressed a little Reed.
"Dear friend, you know you never will succeed
in life if you don't learn to pay attention
to your *appearance*, and if I may mention
it, your *posture*! Always bowing down to plead
for mercy like a common roadside weed!
The whole thing is beyond my comprehension!"
"Oh no," replied the Reed, "I do not chafe
under my fortune down here in the clover
for I can bend and let the wind pass over
when hurricanes approach, and so keep safe,
while *you*, dear friend, may find your bluster dwindling
when torn up by your roots and smashed to kindling."

THE NORTH WIND
AND THE SUN

An unsuspecting traveler on the road
became the subject of an argument
between the Sun and North Wind, each intent
on proving that his customary mode
of power was the more effective goad.
The pair devised a bold experiment,
agreeing that the crown would be bestowed
on whoever who could disrobe that hapless gent.
The North Wind fiercely rose to the occasion,
blowing and blustering with all his might;
the Sun shone gently, shedding warmth and light,
relying on the power of persuasion.
And sure enough, the man decided whereas
the day was hot, he might as well go bare-ass.

THE HARES AND THE LIONS

"We hold these truths to be elementary,"
a group of Hares harangued the mutinous crowd.
"For much too long we animals have allowed
Lions and Wolves and other landed gentry
to rule society, and bar our entry
to the inalienable rights we were endowed
by our Creator! Let us not be cowed!
What we need is a system parliamentary!"
Borne along by freedom's clarion cry
the frenzied crowd besieged the Lion's den,
shouting "Death to Tyrants!" Ah, but then
the Lion showed himself and made reply:
"Observe, dear friends, that those who make the laws
are usually well equipped with teeth and claws."

THE SALT MERCHANT AND HIS DONKEY

A Donkey tripped and fell into a stream
while carrying a heavy load of salt
to market from a Merchant's storage vault.
The Donkey thought "It's odd in the extreme
that, when they're wet, these bags of salt all seem
to weigh much less! The plunge was not my fault,
but now I've learned the trick, and find it all
too easy to repeat this simple scheme!"
And so the ass contrived to make the same
plunge into water every market day
until the Merchant hit upon a way
to beat the schemer at his little game.
Next time the foolish Donkey took a plunge his
cargo was (*surprise!*) not salt but sponges.

THE VIXEN AND
THE LIONESS

A Lioness was taunted by a Vixen
out for an airing on a summer day.
"I see you've got one cub, and I daresay
you're green with jealousy about the six in
my litter," sneered the fox, getting her licks in
against her rival. "I'm happy to convey
congratulations — but now just back away,"
replied the Lioness, "and please don't mix in
my business!" "Pooh! Why give yourself such airs?"
the Vixen scoffed. "One solitary cub
while *I* have six – enough to start a club!"
The Lioness answered, "When it comes to heirs
it's true I only have a single scion,
but just remember, *that one is a lion.*"

THE THREE
TRADESMEN

A thriving city found itself surrounded
by hostile troops, and rushed to build walls thick
enough to save its people in the nick
of time. Panic ensued! The streets resounded
with shouts, until the mayor's gavel pounded.
"Let each man speak," he said, "and then we'll pick
the wisest plan." "It stands to reason brick
is best for walls," the bricklayers propounded.
Carpenters argued, "No! The wisest choice is
timber!" Tanners claimed, "In cold and rainy weather
you'll find the best defense is well-tanned leather."
And so with selfish goals and strident voices
they argued while their city was invaded.
(Self-interest and stupidity betrayed it.)

Three Tradesmen

THE WOODSMAN
AND THE SERPENT

The dark shape lying frozen in the snow
turned out to be a dying rattlesnake.
Feeling pity for the creature's sake
(the temperature was 42 below!)
a passing Woodsman took it home to show
his children. This was likely a mistake!
Warmed by the fire, the Serpent came awake;
the children watched its head move to and fro . . .
"Look Daddy, look!" the youngest daughter said,
"we've saved its life!" Baring its fangs to strike
the Serpent lunged right at the helpless tyke!
Grabbing an axe, the man cut off its head!
A moment later, he'd have had a sick kid —
(he should have known there's no thanks from the wicked).

THE SWAN AND
THE GOOSE

A rich man kept a white Swan and a Goose,
one for his looks, the other for the table.
They shared a cozy corner of the stable.
One night the cook, holding a silken noose
with which to snare some poultry for his use
at dinnertime, found he wasn't able
to tell the two apart (in Aesop's fable
the darkness of the night was his excuse).
Things for the Swan were going very wrong!
The soup was hot and bubbling on the fire,
his lease on life was ready to expire
when from his throat there burst his dying song.
"That don't sound right," the cook said, "wait a sec!"
The moral is "Speak up, and save your neck."

 # THE HUNTER AND
THE WOODSMAN

Searching the forest for a lion's tracks,
a Hunter met some Woodsmen felling oaks.
In the haughty tone reserved for gentlefolks
addressing those who wield a workman's axe,
the Hunter said, "My wall of trophies lacks
a lion's head — have any of you blokes
seen his footprints here?" "No need to coax
us, sir," replied a Woodsman, "he attacks
our livestock, so we'll take you to his lair!"
At this the Hunter's teeth began to chatter.
"My goodness," said the Woodsman, "what's the matter?"
"Perhaps I didn't make my question clear,"
the Hunter gasped. "I asked for signs of fresh
footprints of lions, not lions in the flesh!!"

THE TWO FRIENDS
AND THE AXE

"Today's my lucky day! I found an Axe
here in the road!" said Cletus to his friend.
"Nay," replied Sophus, "if you please, amend
your statement, since your formulation lacks
consideration, and skips essential facts!
We're walking here *together*, so I contend
WE found the object, and I would defend
my right to share the prize!" "Okay, relax!
Have it your way!" Cletus then replied.
But as they traveled onward with the loot
the owner of the Axe, in hot pursuit,
fell on them, with eye toward homicide.
"Uh-oh," said Cletus then, "I think we're screwed!"
"WE?" Sophus asked, "To whom do you allude?"

THE FOX AND
THE CAT

Boasted the Fox: "I know a thousand tricks
with which I easily outwit my foes –
the hunters and their hounds. You don't suppose
I'm scared of them! In fact, I get my kicks
from running rings around the local hicks,
raiding the henhouse right beneath the nose
of some poor farmer while his watchdogs doze
and making off with all the plumpest chicks!"
"I really envy you!" the Cat said, "Gee!
I only know *one* trick! I guess I'm dumb!
I'd better do it now, though! Here they come!"
At which she nimbly scampered up a tree.
Meanwhile the Fox, confused by indecision,
was quickly seized and carried off to prison.

The Fox & the Cat

THE SILKWORM AND THE SPIDER

A Silkworm, toiling busily at her loom
to make a wedding dress, found that a Spider
had crawled into position right beside her,
hiring the adjacent weaving room.
The Spider quickly spun a vast volume
of sticky threads, pausing just to chide her
busy neighbor, "Observe! My skein is wider
and twice as long as yours! The bride and groom
will certainly choose my outfit for their marriage!"
"Hush up!" the Silkworm said, "True art takes time
and labor, but the product is sublime;
and (though of course it pains me to disparage
your work) we'll see whose weaving takes the prize,
mine with exquisite threads, yours with dead flies."

THE MULE

"My father surely was a racing steed,"
a frisky Mule proclaimed while running wild
in a green pasture, "and I am his child
in looks, in heart, in spirit, and in speed."
A Mule, you must know, is the mongrel seed
of horse and donkey, oftentimes reviled
as stubborn, headstrong, and too quickly riled
by insults to his parentage or breed.
Next day, the Mule's brief holiday was over.
His master piled a huge and heavy stack
of goods for market on his sturdy back.
He grumbled, "When I frolicked in the clover
I thought myself a horse, but now, alas,
I'm pretty sure my father was an ass."

THE LION AND
THE STATUE

A drunken man addressed a Lion thus:
"In any kind of battle I could match you
my wits against your muscle and dispatch you."
The Lion countered, "Of the two of us
I am the stronger and more agile, plus
I have these deadly claws with which to scratch you."
"You're wrong, my friend! Behold this marble Statue
depicting Hercules in arduous
combat with a Lion? Observe who's winning!"
the man declared, "I guess that proves my case!"
"*Not so!* It only proves the human race
is quite adept at what is known as 'spinning'.
The one who carves the Statue, don't you see,
depicts things as he wishes them to be."

HPKOYΛI

THE CUB AND
THE KITTEN

A Bear Cub and a Kitten became friends,
One day the poor Cub realized he was smitten —
madly in love with his dear friend the Kitten!
"What am I to do to make amends
for this forbidden passion? It offends
good sense to think a great big Bear could fit in
a small cat's life, or she in mine —'tis written
'Like with Like', and so our story ends."
But wait! Time passed, the Cub became a Bear;
one day as he was strolling through the wildwood
he turned his head and saw her standing there,
the well-remembered Kitten from his childhood:
a graceful Panther now, the image of
the truth she uttered: *"Never fear to love."*

THE NURSE AND
THE WOLF

The whining of the child upon her lap
drove a kindly Nurse to an extreme
reaction. "Stop your whining or I'll scream!
If you don't quiet down and take your nap
I'll throw you to the wolves before I snap!"
Now it happened that a Wolf, his eyes agleam
was passing by the window. "It's a dream
come true!" he thought, "am I a lucky chap!"
Pretty soon the child began to sniffle,
the Wolf came forward then, with tail awag,
"I'm ready, toss him out!" The Nurse said "*Piffle!*"
Get out of here, and fast, you old fleabag!
You're crazy to believe a word I've spoken,
for enemies' vows are made just to be broken!"

THE FROGS ASKING
FOR A KING

"All of your creatures have a King but us!"
complained the Frogs to father Zeus one day.
"Mammals bow to Lions; birds, they say,
revere the Eagle, human beings fuss
over their Kings, but we amphibious
life forms have no sovereign to obey!"
Taking advantage of their naiveté,
and being much too busy to discuss
the matter further, Zeus tossed down a log
into their swamp. *"Frogs, behold your King!"*
But soon the Frogs came back, petitioning
for a more lively monarch in the bog.
Annoyed that they had ventured to complain
Zeus gave them what they asked — a hungry Crane.

THE MAN, THE BOY, AND THE DONKEY

"You fools, why keep a Donkey you don't ride?"
a townsman asked a farmer and his son
walking to town with their companion,
an old decrepit Donkey, by their side.
"He's right," the farmer thought, *"Son, sit astride*
the Donkey." But as soon as that was done
a woman jeered, *"Look at that lazy one*
who makes his father walk! Has he no pride?"
"She's right," the farmer thought, "there's no excuse
for that!" so son and father traded places.
But then a crowd converged with angry faces,
shouting *"For shame! This looks like child abuse!"*
"Then sit beside me, son, we'll ride together,"
the man said, but the Donkey, overloaded
(since neither one was lighter than a feather!)
fell on its face the moment that they rode it.
"Alas," declared the father to his son
as they carried the Donkey home, *"please all, please none!"*

SONNETS FROM AESOP ALPHABETICAL INDEX

Androcles and lion **16**

Ant and chrysalis **144**

Ant and dove **94**

Ant and grasshopper **126**

Ass and his shadow **8**

Ass and mule **40**

Belling the cat **4**

Boasting traveler **56**

Boy and the cookies **50**

Boy bathing **62**

Boy who cried wolf **146**

Bundle of sticks **30**

Cat and Venus **138**

City mouse & country mouse **68**

Crab and her son **34**

Crow and pitcher **88**

Cub and kitten **194**

Dog and his reflection **46**

Dog and wolf **118**

Dog in the manger **28**

Dog's house **82**

Donkey and horse **80**

Donkey and lapdog **116**

Donkey and wolf **32**

Eagle and arrow **52**

Eagle and hawk **18**

Farmer and his sons **66**

Fisherman and the fish **84**

Flea and ox **70**

Fox and cat **186**

Fox and crane **114**

Fox and crow **78**

Fox, cock and dog **2**

Fox and lion **98**

Fox and grapes **14**

Fox who lost his tail **150**

Frogs and well **64**

Frogs asking for a king **198**

Gluttonous fox **42**

Goatherd and wild goats **24**

Hare and hound **92**

Hare and tortoise **152**

Hares and lions **170**

Hercules and Athena **74**

Hercules and wagon driver **128**

Horse and his rider **148**

Horse, deer, and man **130**

Hunter and woodsman **182**

Kingdom of lion **90**

Lark and her young ones **124**

Lark burying her father **106**

Lion and boar **112**

Lion and mouse **48**

Lion in love **134**

Lion, fox, and ass **72**

Lion, fox, and beasts **158**

SONNETS FROM AESOP ALPHABETICAL INDEX

Lion and Statue **192**

Man and two sweethearts **38**

Man, boy, and donkey **200**

Milkmaid and her pail **156**

Miser **110**

Mule **190**

North wind and sun **168**

Nurse and wolf **196**

Old man and Death **120**

Old woman and physician **102**

Oxen and axletrees **136**

Peacock and crane **44**

Peasant and eagle **164**

Pig, sheep, and goat **58**

Rabbit and frogs **108**

Rabbit with many friends **36**

Rooster and jewel **60**

Salt merchant and donkey **172**

Serpent and file **104**

Seller of images **76**

Shepherd and sea **10**

Shipwrecked sailors **26**

Sick stag **154**

Silkworm and spider **188**

Stag and hunter **100**

Stag and vine **162**

Swan and goose **180**

Three tradesmen **176**

Traveler and Fortune **160**

Tree and reed **166**

Trees under protection of gods **132**

Two daughters **96**

Two friends and axe **184**

Two friends and bear **12**

Two pots **22**

Vixen and lioness **174**

Wolf and crane **6**

Wolf and goat **122**

Wolf and kid **140**

Wolf and sheep **54**

Wolf, fox, and ape **86**

Wolf in sheep's clothing **20**

Woodsman and nightingale **142**

Woodsman and serpent **178**

JUDITH GOLDHABER is a poet, playwright, science writer, and journalist. Her poems have appeared in the National Poetry Review, Astropoetica, the Literary Review, the Susquehanna Quarterly, and Byline. In 2004 she won first prize in the National Poetry Review's poetry competition and in the "In the Beginning was the Word" poetry contest, and was a finalist in five other national competitions. As a playwright, she has written the book and lyrics for two musicals based on the lives of great individuals in modern science. Her musical about Stephen Hawking, Falling Through a Hole in the Air, received a $5,000 grant from Paul Newman's "Newman's Own" Foundation. Her new musical, Johnnie & Dollie, is about Einstein's "lost" daughter Lieserl. In addition to Sonnets from Aesop, she is the author of The Garden Spider and Naming the Winds.

GERSON GOLDHABER is professor of physics in the graduate school at the University of California, Berkeley, and an artist who has worked in many media. His previous publications have been in the field of experimental particle physics and astrophysics. He is co-author of The Experimental Foundations of Particle Physics, and has written or co-authored over 250 papers reporting his research on elementary particles and cosmology. He is a member of the U.S. National Academy of Sciences, a fellow of the American Academy of Arts and Sciences, a Guggenheim fellow, and a foreign member of the Royal Swedish Academy of Sciences. He was named California Scientist of the Year in 1977, and is a winner of the Panofsky Prize of the American Physical Society.

Sonnets from Aesop is the first collaboration between the couple, not counting their children and grandchildren.